D1532111

The **STEM** of

Bridges and Tunnels

By Kristin Thiel

Cavendish
Square

New York

Published in 2021 by Cavendish Square Publishing, LLC
243 5th Avenue, Suite 136, New York, NY 10016

Copyright © 2021 by Cavendish Square Publishing, LLC

First Edition

Website: cavendishsq.com

This publication represents the opinions and views of the author based on his or her personal experience, knowledge, and research. The information in this book serves as a general guide only. The author and publisher have used their best efforts in preparing this book and disclaim liability rising directly or indirectly from the use and application of this book.

All websites were available and accurate when this book was sent to press.

Library of Congress Cataloging-in-Publication Data

Names: Thiel, Kristin, 1977- author.
Title: The STEM of bridges and tunnels / Kristin Thiel.
Other titles: Bridges and tunnels
Description: First edition. | New York : Cavendish Square, [2021] | Series: The world of STEM | Includes bibliographical references and index.
Identifiers: LCCN 2019042273 (print) | LCCN 2019042274 (ebook) | ISBN 9781502650108 (library binding) | ISBN 9781502650085 (paperback) | ISBN 9781502650092 (set) | ISBN 9781502650115 (ebook)
Subjects: LCSH: Bridges–Juvenile literature. | Tunnels–Juvenile literature.
Classification: LCC TG148 .T54 2021 (print) | LCC TG148 (ebook) | DDC 624.1/93–dc23
LC record available at https://lccn.loc.gov/2019042273
LC ebook record available at https://lccn.loc.gov/2019042274

Editor: Caitlyn Miller and Jennifer Lombardo
Copy Editor: Alex Tessman
Designer: Andrea Davison-Bartolotta

The photographs in this book are used by permission and through the courtesy of: Cover, p. 1 Songquan Deng/Shutterstock.com; series art (texture) bestbrk/Shutterstock.com; p. 4 aaabbbccc/Shutterstock.com; p. 7 Westend61/Getty Images; p. 8 Pe3k/Shutterstock.com; p. 9 Iain Masterton/Canopy/Getty Images Plus/Getty Images; p. 10 Gervasio S. _ Eureka_89/Shutterstock.com; pp. 12–13 sigurcamp/Shutterstock.com; pp. 14–15 ESB Professional/Shutterstock.com; p. 17 (bottom) Adazhiy Dmytro/Shutterstock.com; p. 17 (top) Grand Warszawski/Shutterstock.com; p. 18 Aleksandr Yu/Shutterstock.com; p. 20 ventdusud/Shutterstock.com; p. 22 Adwo/Shutterstock.com; p. 23 Chris Hyde/Shutterstock.com; p. 24 Sundry Photography/Shutterstock.com; p. 27 Eric Broder Van Dyke/Shutterstock.com; p. 28 Scott Sonner/AP Images; p. 29 cleanfotos/Shutterstock.com.

Some of the images in this book illustrate individuals who are models. The depictions do not imply actual situations or events.

CPSIA compliance information: Batch #CS20CSQ: For further information contact Cavendish Square Publishing LLC, New York, New York at 1-877-980-4450.

Printed in the United States of America

Find us on

Contents

THE BASICS OF BRIDGES AND TUNNELS

1

You may have built a bridge with school supplies in science class. You may have dug tunnels through sand or snow while playing. Many people travel across bridges and through tunnels every day. Bridges and tunnels are very common. They're also examples of **STEM** at work.

Why Do We Use Bridges and Tunnels?

Bridges allow people to cross **unstable** ground. Tunnels help people travel through mountains. Tunnels also bring in fresh water for drinking and carry dirty water away from a city. Both bridges

You probably use bridges and tunnels a lot, but do you know what keeps them up?

and tunnels help people cross water. They also help people move supplies long distances.

People use bridges and tunnels for many reasons. Bridges and tunnels help connect communities, but they can also be used to divide communities. In addition, bridges and tunnels have been used during wars throughout history. Military leaders can use bridges and tunnels to reach their enemies quickly. They can also destroy bridges and tunnels to keep enemies out.

THINK ON YOUR OWN

What's a problem that building a tunnel would help you solve?

The History of Bridges and Tunnels

Humans started using bridges and tunnels thousands of years ago. They often made simple bridges out of logs to cross water. One of the oldest bridges still in use is in Greece. The bridge is made of stones. It was built between 1300 and 1190 BCE.

Arkadiko Bridge (shown here) in Greece is more than 700 years old.

People in what's now Iran created some of the world's first tunnels, called qanats. They carried water for farms. Some qanats are 2,700 years old! The first underwater tunnel was the Thames Tunnel, which was built between 1825 and 1843 in the United Kingdom.

This qanat moves water under Shafiabad, Iran.

The Power of STEM

Today, people study hard to become engineers—people who use STEM to solve problems. They design, or plan, bridges and tunnels. They use math and science to make sure what they design won't **collapse**.

Statics

Bridge engineers and tunnel engineers must understand statics. Statics is part of a branch of science called **physics**. Statics deals with forces that act on things that are standing still. Forces can push on something. Forces can also pull on something. Both bridges and tunnels must stay strong against many forces.

Bridges and tunnels must support dead load. That's the weight of the bridge or tunnel by itself. Bridges and tunnels must support living load too. That's the weight of the people and vehicles traveling on or through them. These forces are always present. If a bridge or tunnel hasn't collapsed, it's holding strong against all those forces.

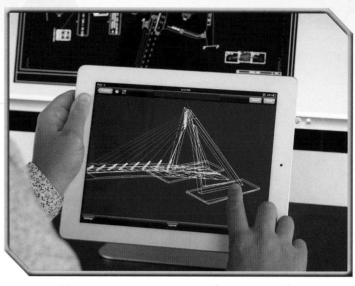

Using computers to design and test bridges saves money and time.

THINK ON YOUR OWN

Why might a bridge fall apart during a storm?

NEW DESIGNS

2

Bridge and tunnel engineering has changed over time. Changes in **materials**, technology, and needs have led to new ideas. These ideas have made bridges stronger, and they've made tunnels that go through different kinds of places—even under water!

Arch Bridges

Arch bridges are a strong style of ancient bridge. The ancient Romans were famous for their arch bridges. They built bridges almost 2,000 years ago that are still standing. They used stones.

◀ ·············

Some aquariums use tunnels to help visitors feel closer to the underwater world.

The arch shape and the stones make these bridges very strong. The Romans didn't even have to use mortar to stick the stones together. Mortar is a mix of materials that hardens when it dries. Forces have held Roman bridges together without mortar.

THINK ON YOUR OWN

Why are some ancient bridges still standing? Why have some collapsed?

Shown here is the Pont du Gard, which was built by the ancient Romans.

Changes in Bridge Materials

Today's materials are even stronger than stone. Steel can make much bigger arches than stone can. This creates longer, stronger bridges. However, steel costs more than stone. The prices for iron and coal, which are used to make steel, keep going up. Steel is also worse for the **environment** than stone. Making steel pollutes the air and water. That's why engineers are working to find new materials to use.

The New River Gorge Bridge in West Virginia is the third highest steel bridge in the United States.

Tunnel Inventions

Many tunnels are made out of whatever material they cut through, such as clay and rock, which have been used for thousands of years. Tunnels that go under water, however, can cause big problems. The bed, or ground, under water is very soft and unstable.

The invention of the tunneling shield in 1818 let engineers build underwater tunnels for the first time. The inventor was **inspired** by the shipworm. The shipworm's shell helps it drill through wood and push the sawdust it made out behind it. The tunneling shield does the same thing with mud. This keeps the tunnel from filling back in before it's finished. Tunneling shields look different today, but they're still used.

THINK ON YOUR OWN

Why is the ground under water different than the ground in other places?

Machines that dig tunnels act like moles. They dig out the dirt to make things such as subway tunnels.

17

About 150,000 bridges in the United States need big repairs. Some have fallen apart. One was a bridge across the Mississippi River in Minneapolis, Minnesota. There were a lot of cars and trucks on it when it fell in 2007.

Engineers have studied these bridges. They found problems with their designs. They also found **damage** to the bridges. Other bridges have been standing for years. Engineers look at the differences between these bridges and the damaged ones. This helps them make better ones in the future.

◀ ⋯⋯⋯⋯⋯

Fixing bridges takes a lot of time and work, but it's important to keep people safe.

An Engineering Marvel

The Golden Gate Bridge in California is an old bridge. However, the bridge's design is still good. It had only minor damage after a strong earthquake in 1989. It's a good example of old STEM ideas that can still be used to build bridges and tunnels today. It's also interesting to think about how engineers would use new STEM ideas to make it even stronger today.

The Golden Gate Bridge connects the city of San Francisco with Marin County in California. It was built between 1933 and 1937. The Golden Gate Bridge was

The Golden Gate Bridge is one of the most famous bridges in the world.

the longest suspension bridge in the world until 1964. That year, a longer bridge was built in New York City.

What Is a Suspension Bridge?

Suspension bridges are both useful and beautiful. That makes them a top choice for many engineers. Modern suspension bridges have two main parts. They have cables and towers. These bridges work because two forces balance each other. **Tension** on the wire cables is equal to **compression** on the towers. The bridge's road hangs from suspenders. These are connected to main cables. The first suspension bridges had cables made of woven plant material. Later suspension bridges had iron cables. The Golden Gate Bridge has cables made with 80,000 miles (128,748 kilometers) of steel wire.

Math and Modeling

There were no computers when suspension bridges were invented. Engineers used **slide rules**, pencils, and paper to do the math needed to plan these bridges. They tested their math. They did this by making a steel model of the bridge.

Geologists also helped. Geologists are scientists who study Earth. They found out if the nearby rock could support, or hold, the bridge's weight. Geologists used a model as a test. They put a lot of weight on a tiny square of rock. This helped them know if more rock would support a whole bridge.

Geologists help engineers make sure a new bridge will be safe.

THINK ON YOUR OWN

What are some other tests scientists can do to make sure a bridge will work before they build it?

New Materials and Technology

Today's engineers might make a bridge like the Golden Gate Bridge from different materials. They might use fiber reinforced polymers (FRPs). FRPs are lighter and stronger than steel. They wouldn't wear away in the damp San Francisco air.

THINK ON YOUR OWN

Why didn't the people who built the Golden Gate Bridge use fiber reinforced polymers (FRPs)?

The bridge decks of Dragon Bridge in Wales (shown here) are made of FRPs.

ENGINEERING THE FUTURE

Bridges and tunnels are going to keep changing in many ways. There are always new materials and new ideas. These will help engineers build stronger bridges and tunnels. In the future, bridges may not collapse in earthquakes. New ideas also help bridges and tunnels meet big goals. For example, tunnels might cut down on road traffic.

Bridges Standing Strong in Earthquakes

Earthquakes shake the ground. They can also damage whatever is built above the ground.

The Robin Williams Tunnel allows cars to easily get through the hills between Marin County and the Golden Gate Bridge in California.

Bridges can be damaged in earthquakes. Modern bridges shouldn't collapse during an earthquake. However, that doesn't mean they're safe to use. They may look fine, but they might be weakened. The ramps leading on and off the bridges may also be damaged. Engineers hope to change this with new materials.

Materials with Memory

In February 2019, a new bridge opened in Seattle, Washington. It's the world's first bridge made of metals and **concrete** that bend. This bridge won't just sway in a major earthquake. Instead, it will snap back to its original shape on its own.

THINK ON YOUR OWN

Why do people worry about bridges getting damaged in earthquakes?

Cranes work on tearing down part of a bridge in Seattle, Washington, so it can be rebuilt with new materials.

The metal used to make this bridge is called shape-memory alloy (SMA). It's a mix of the metals titanium and nickel. It "remembers" its original shape and returns to it. The concrete is called engineered cementitious concrete (ECC). It's full of special fibers that control cracking.

The Earthquake Engineering Lab at the University of Nevada, Reno, spent 15 years testing the bridge using models. They used something called a shake table to create "earthquakes" in the lab!

A shake table (shown here) shakes like the ground would in an earthquake. This is one way engineers test bridge designs.

Tunnels and Traffic

Some problems aren't as harmful as earthquakes. Problems like traffic jams happen every day. Traffic is getting worse in many cities. Some people think tunnels will help.

Building tunnels underground helps communities. When roads are being worked on above ground, people have to take new routes. That can cause bad traffic during construction. Building tunnels underground often doesn't cause these problems.

Many people think roads in tunnels are a good idea. There are just a few problems. Right now, building tunnels takes too long and costs too much. Engineers are trying to solve these problems. They think we need more research and testing. Then maybe tunnels can be the way most people get around.

Tunnels may help spread out traffic during busy travel times.

THINK ON YOUR OWN

How can we make building tunnels faster and cheaper?

Glossary

collapse To fall completely and suddenly.

compression A force that squeezes objects.

concrete A building material made from broken stone, sand, cement, and water.

damage Harm done to a person or piece of property. Also, to cause harm to a person or piece of property.

environment The natural world around us.

inspire To move someone to do something great.

material Something from which something else can be made.

physics A branch of science that studies matter, energy, and how they interact.

slide rule A special ruler that helps people multiply and divide quickly.

STEM Science, technology, engineering, and math.

tension A force that pulls on objects.

unstable Likely to shift, crumble, or break apart.

Find Out More

Books

Dougherty, Rachel. *Secret Engineer: How Emily Roebling Built the Brooklyn Bridge*. New York, NY: Roaring Brook Press, 2019.

Moore, Jeanette, and Mike Crosier. *Tunnels! With 25 Science Projects for Kids*. White River Junction, VT: Nomad Press, 2018.

Websites

Building Big
pbs.org/wgbh/buildingbig
The PBS Building Big website offers a lot of information on bridges and tunnels. Click through the many links to learn a lot about both kinds of structures.

History of Bridges
historyofbridges.com
Learn more about how bridges have changed over time.

Index